Fearfully and Wonderfully Made

Written and illustrated by
SABRINA ADEWUMI

Thank you for purchasing an authorized copy of this book and for complying with copyright laws by not reproducing in any form without permission.
Copyright © 2023 All Rights Reserved

Scripture quotations marked AMP are taken from the Amplified® Bible (AMP), Copyright © 2015 by The Lockman Foundation. Used by permission. lockman.org

For our three little birds,

and children everywhere, may you grow to know Your

Creator and who He created you to be.

Long before
I was even born
God had me in His mind

He could have made my eyes

blue,

or

green

But, He chose to make them

brown

instead.

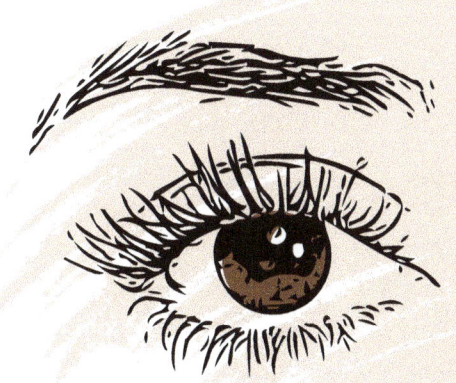
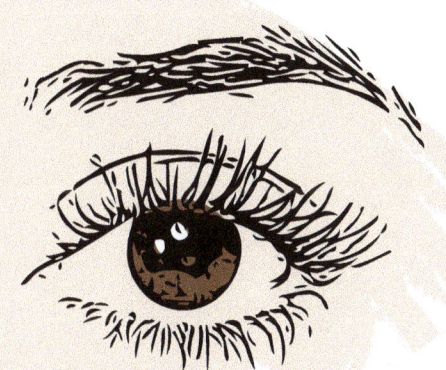

Like an artist,
He looked at all the colors

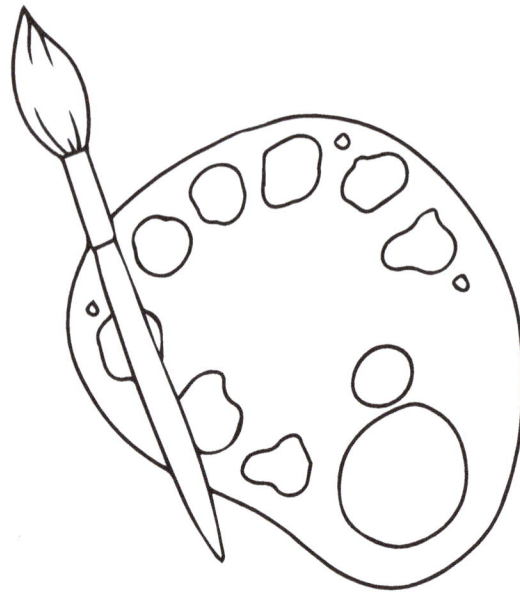

and then

He gave my skin the perfect shade

So I don't compare my skin to anyone else, because...

My favorite foods

and things to do

Spelling tests make me feel queasy

But I'm really good at playing chess

And I make basketball look easy!

(and you probably wouldn't ask me for a serenade)

But if there's one thing I know for sure - it's this...

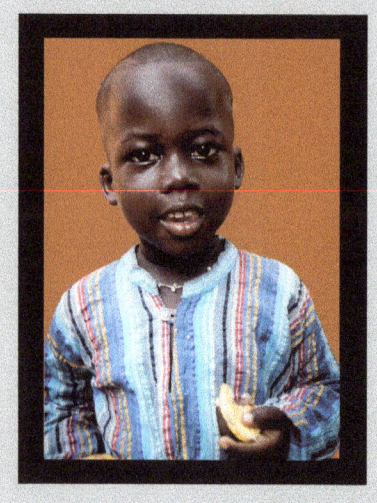  

Like a beautiful masterpiece that belongs

 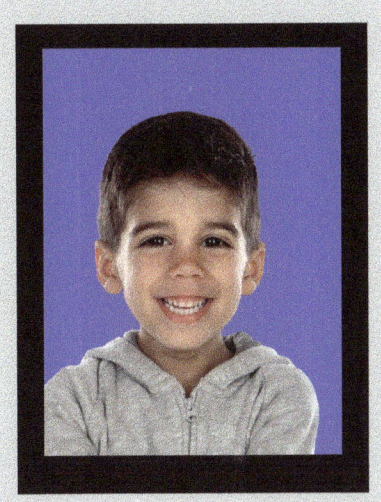 

in a museum or famous art gallery

Extraordinarily complex and WONDERFUL

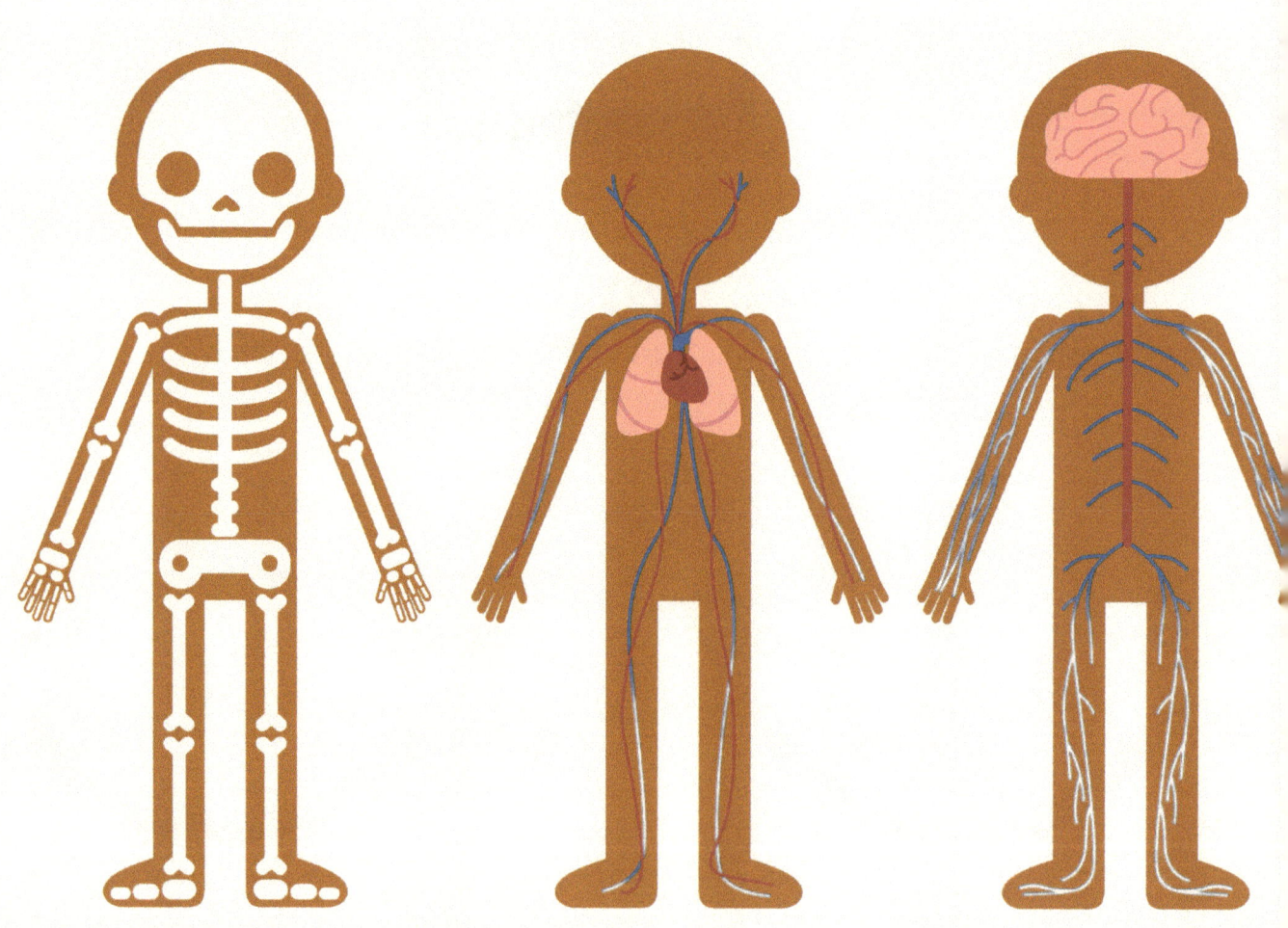

God's handiwork-

That's me!

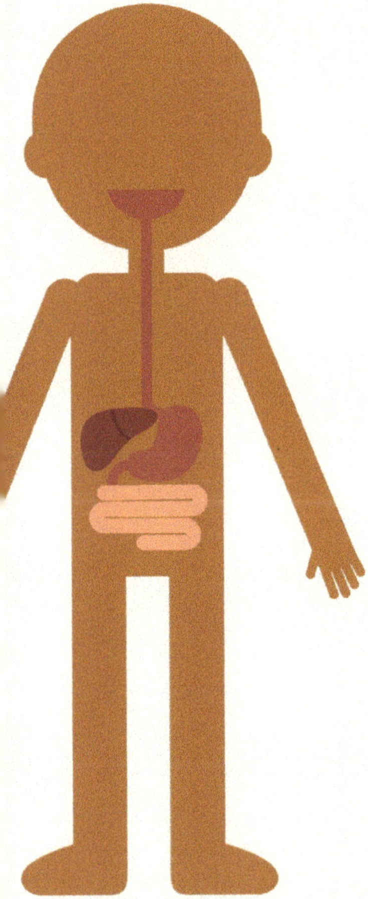

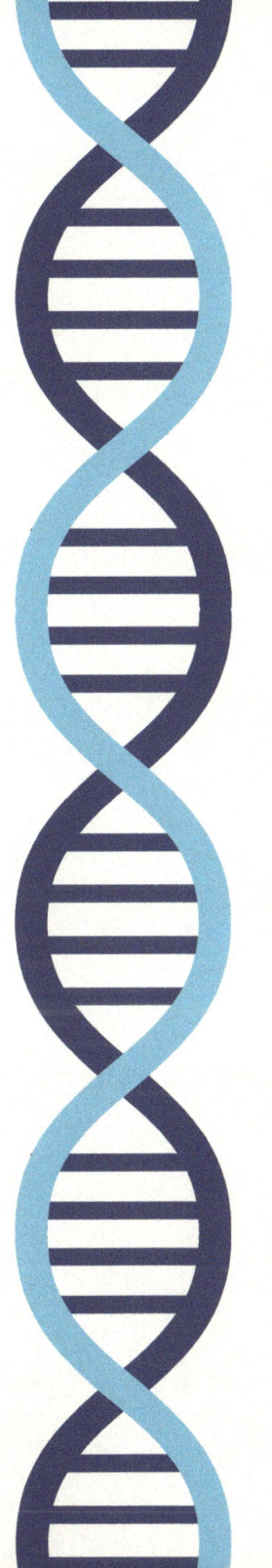

So next time you're feeling **insecure**

Or something makes you feel **afraid**

fULLy And

Ly MAdE

I will give thanks and praise to You, for I am fearfully and wonderfully made; Wonderful are Your works, And my soul knows it very well.

PSALM 139:14 (AMP)

www.ingramcontent.com/pod-product-compliance
Lightning Source LLC
Chambersburg PA
CBHW051402110526
44592CB00023B/2922